NEBRASKA

NEBRASKA

HELLO
U.S.A.

by A. P. Porter

Lerner Publications Company

You'll find this picture of blue agate at the beginning of each chapter in this book. Blue agate has been the state gemstone of Nebraska since 1967. At Nebraska's Agate Fossil Beds National Monument, layers of agate rock contain many ancient fossils. Agates are often used to make jewelry because of their beautiful colors.

Cover (left): Sandhill cranes on the Platte River at sunset. Cover (right): Nebraska Cornhuskers football game. Pages 2–3: The White River Badlands. Page 3: Brown and white Hereford calf.

This book is available in two editions:
Library binding by Lerner Publications Company, a division of Lerner Publishing Group
Soft cover by First Avenue Editions, an imprint of Lerner Publishing Group
241 First Avenue North
Minneapolis, MN 55401 U.S.A.

Website address: www.lernerbooks.com

Library of Congress Cataloging-in-Publication Data

Porter, A. P.
    Nebraska / by A. P. Porter.— Rev. and expanded 2nd ed.
       p.   cm. — (Hello U.S.A.)
    Summary: Introduces the geography, history, people, industries, and other highlights of Nebraska.
    Includes bibliographical references and index.
    ISBN: 0–8225–4093–2 (lib. bdg. : alk. paper)
    ISBN: 0–8225–0786–2 (pbk. : alk. paper)
    1. Nebraska—Juvenile literature. [1. Nebraska.] I. Title. II. Series.
F666.3 .P67 2003
978.2—dc21   2001008652

Manufactured in the United States of America
1 2 3 4 5 6 – JR – 08 07 06 05 04 03

CONTENTS

Prairie grasses are abundant in Nebraska's Rainwater Basin.

THE LAND

Great Plains

Most of Nebraska is part of the Great Plains—a large, flat region in central North America. Before people lived on the earth, the Great Plains were the floor of a shallow sea that formed when **glaciers**—huge, slow-moving sheets of ice—in the area melted.

Long after the sea dried up, the Oto Indians named the river that crossed through the region *nebrathka*, which means "flat water." French explorers used their word for "flat" when they called that flat water the Platte River.

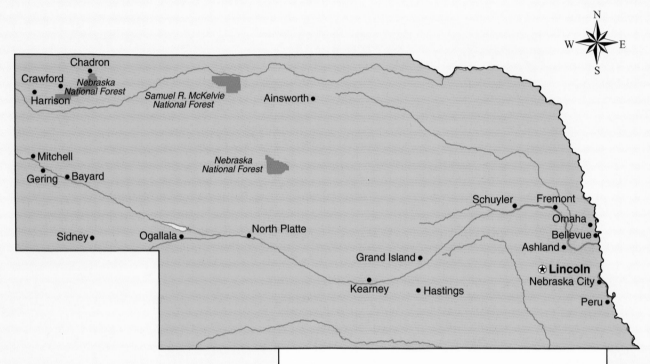

NEBRASKA
Political Map

⊛ State capital

0	25	50 Miles

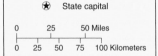

The drawing of Nebraska on this page is called a political map. It shows features created by people, including cities, railways, and parks. The map on the facing page is called a physical map. It shows physical features of Nebraska, such as islands, mountains, rivers, and lakes. The colors represent a range of elevations, or heights above sea level (see legend box). This map also shows the geographical regions of Nebraska.

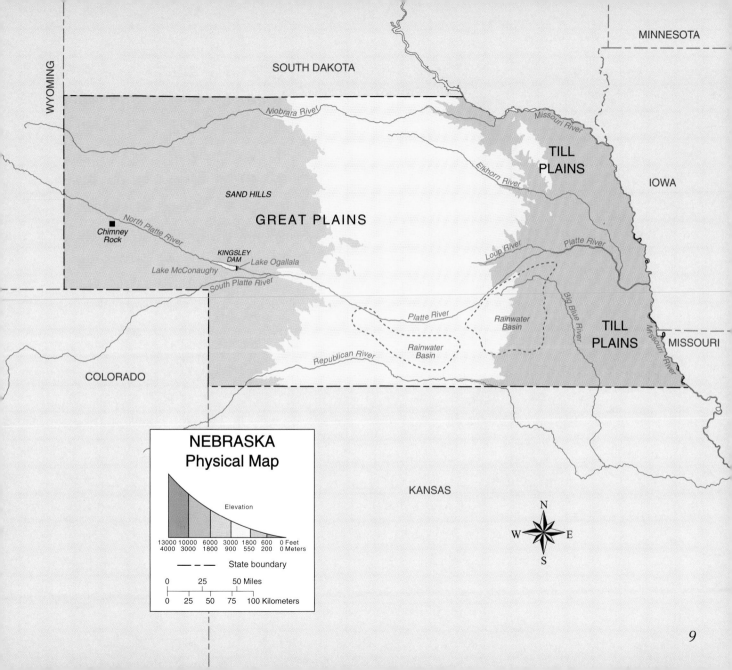

WYOMING

SOUTH DAKOTA

MINNESOTA

Niobrara River

Missouri River

TILL
PLAINS

IOWA

SAND HILLS

GREAT PLAINS

Elkhorn River

North Platte River

*Chimney
Rock*

KINGSLEY
DAM   *Lake Ogallala*

Lake McConaughy

Loup River

Platte River

South Platte River

Platte River

*Rainwater
Basin*

*Rainwater
Basin*

Republican River

Big Blue River

TILL
PLAINS

Missouri River

MISSOURI

COLORADO

KANSAS

NEBRASKA
Physical Map

Elevation

| 13000 | 10000 | 6000 | 3000 | 1800 | 600 | 0 Feet |
| 4000 | 3000 | 1800 | 900 | 550 | 200 | 0 Meters |

- - -   State boundary

0   25   50 Miles

0   25   50   75   100 Kilometers

N
W   E
S

Although the Platte River is too shallow to navigate, its valley provides a stretch of flatland that is good for railroads, highways, and farming.

The wide, flat Platte River oozes slowly eastward through Nebraska farmland. It collects the flow of the Loup and Elkhorn Rivers along the way. Eventually the Platte flows into the Missouri River, which borders Nebraska on the east. The Niobrara, the Republican, and the Big Blue Rivers also find their way into the Missouri.

Across the Missouri River are the states of Missouri and Iowa. To Nebraska's north is South Dakota, and Wyoming is to the west. Colorado takes a chunk out of Nebraska's southwestern corner. Kansas lies to the south.

Two land regions—the Till Plains and the Great Plains—make up Nebraska. Both regions are

Many farmers in the Till Plains grow corn.

considered **prairie,** or grassland, but the Till Plains get more rain and are more fertile than the Great Plains.

The Till Plains stretch along the Missouri River, covering one-fifth of the state. The glaciers that once inched across this region in eastern Nebraska dragged particles of clay, sand, and rock along the ground. Called **till,** the debris was strewn across the Till Plains by the glaciers.

Over time, **loess** (windblown dust) combined with the till to form the rich soil that feeds prairie grasses on the Till Plains. Till and loess also have made the Till Plains excellent for growing crops.

West of the Till Plains, the mostly treeless Great Plains extend westward for more than 400 miles—all the way into Wyoming and Colorado. Grazing cattle and fields of wheat are common sights on the Great Plains.

Hills of sand roll through the center of Nebraska's Great Plains region. Called the Sand Hills, this section is the largest area of sand dunes in the United States. Unlike most other dunes, the Sand Hills are covered with grasses that hold the sand in place. The rich grasses and many streams of the Sand Hills make the area especially good for grazing cattle.

Across the state, dams have been built on rivers to collect water for **hydropower.** The

The Sand Hills are home to Snake River Falls, Nebraska's largest waterfall.

A tornado touches down in a field. These spiraling windstorms can destroy everything in their path.

water is then released to turn wheels that generate electricity. Water held back by the dams creates several of Nebraska's lakes, including Lake McConaughy, the state's biggest. These lakes can also be used to collect floodwaters, which can be released slowly into rivers so they won't flood homes and farms.

Floods are a common threat in Nebraska, where blizzards, hailstorms, and tornadoes lash the plains and prairies most years. At other times, however, **droughts,** or prolonged dry spells, endanger the state's crops and cattle. Weather in Nebraska swings from hot summers to cold winters. Temperatures average 76° F in July and 23° F in January.

In winter, frost clings to the branches of Nebraska's trees.

When European explorers passed through Nebraska, they saw few trees in the region. In the twenty-first century, the Nebraska National Forest is the largest planted forest in the United States. Cottonwood, oak, willow, linden, and ash trees all grow well in Nebraska, especially along riverbanks. Still, only 2 percent of the state is wooded.

Bluestem and other tall prairie grasses grow wild in eastern Nebraska. Grama and buffalo grass need little rain and grow mostly in the west, where less than 20 inches of rain fall each year.

In eastern Nebraska, which gets about 27 inches of rain most years, phlox, violets, and evening primroses greet each spring. Wildflowers such as spiderworts, wild roses, poppies, and blue flags grow well all over the state during the hot summer.

Mule deer, coyotes, skunks, raccoons, and prairie dogs are some of the wild animals found in Nebraska. Ducks, geese, pheasants, quail, and cranes nest mainly in the wet **marshlands** of the Rainwater Basin south of the Platte River.

At one time, millions of bison (buffalo) roamed the Great Plains in Nebraska and other states. Almost all of these animals were killed by white hunters in the late 1800s. The ancestors of the few remaining bison are protected on game preserves.

Nebraska's prairie is home to the black-tailed prairie dog *(above)* and the bull elk *(right)*.

THE HISTORY

Natives and Newcomers

About 10,000 years ago, when the first humans arrived in what later became Nebraska, the region was a green plain. Large, plant-eating animals such as 8-foot moose, sloths the size of elephants, and 14-foot woolly mammoths roamed the region. Meat eaters included the short-faced bear, the dire wolf, and the teratorn, a bird with a 15-foot wingspan.

Early Native Americans, or Indians, of the Great Plains lived in small groups and moved several times a year. Hunters ambushed bison near water holes or drove them over cliffs, killing dozens of animals at a time. The people ate the bison's flesh and used the rest of its parts for clothing, shelter, and tools.

By A.D. 1200, some American Indians were growing squash, beans, and corn in the area that became Nebraska. They also traded furs, hides, and dried meat. Giant dust storms in the 1400s may have forced these people out of the area.

But other groups found their way onto the Great Plains. For centuries the Pawnee farmed and hunted the land that later became Nebraska. The Pawnee, like other Indian groups, had no written language.

More than 10,000 years ago, woolly mammoths lived in the area that later became Nebraska. These giant creatures had tusks that sometimes grew as long as 13 feet!

For their history, they relied on storytellers, who told the next generations about the group's past and added important events from their own lifetimes.

By the 1600s, the Oto, Ponca, Omaha, and Iowa Indians had moved to what became eastern

Millions of bison roamed the grasslands of the Great Plains for centuries.

Indians hunted deer, bear, and bison with spears and arrows. Their weapons had sharp stone points.

Nebraska. They had come from farther east to get away from their enemies and to find food. Like the Pawnee, these newcomers lived in earthen houses and farmed during the summer. The rest of the year they followed herds of bison.

In western Nebraska in the 1600s, the Plains Apache and the Dakota Sioux led a different lifestyle. Rather than farming the land in one place, they spent most of the year on the move, hunting game and gathering wild plants for food.

Hunting bison on horseback was dangerous work. This Indian hunter *(upper left)* could have been trampled if he had slipped off his galloping horse or the running bison.

Horses became the backbone of Indian life on the Great Plains. The animals had strayed north from Spanish settlements in the 1500s. Soon Plains Indians were much more mobile than before. On horses, they could kill more bison. Horses came to mean wealth to these people.

The first white people to cross what later became Nebraska were probably Paul and Pierre Mallet. In 1739 the two brothers walked along the Platte River on their way to the Santa Fe settlement in the Southwest.

At the time, France claimed all the land between

the Mississippi River and the Rocky Mountains—a huge area called Louisiana. But ownership shifted back and forth between France and Spain during the 1600s and 1700s.

Then in 1803, France sold Louisiana to the newly formed United States in a deal called the Louisiana Purchase. Life along the Platte River began to change.

Over the centuries, many explorers have followed the Platte River to western North America.

The following year, Meriwether Lewis and William Clark explored the eastern edge of what would become Nebraska.

Fur traders began living along the Platte and Missouri Rivers in 1807, when Manuel Lisa built a fur-trading post near the site that later became Omaha, Nebraska's biggest city. These merchants brought metal products—arrow tips, pots, pans,

Beginning in the 1700s, Plains Indians acquired glass beads from fur traders, who operated out of trading posts like this one.

Plains Indians sewed beads onto cloth to make colorful designs.

axes, knives—to exchange with the Indians for furs. With these tools available, the Indians stopped making their own arrowheads, pottery, and other tools.

Interacting and trading with white people changed the lives of the Indians in other ways, too. When the traders began selling glass beads, machine-made cloth, and steel needles, Indian women quit using quills and instead sewed the traders' beads onto the traders' fabric. Indian men began to wear blankets instead of buffalo robes.

The Indians in the area knew nothing about the making or effects of alcohol. When bargaining for the finest furs, traders used whiskey to get the Indians drunk. The traders would then cheat the Indians and get rich as a result.

The fur traders also exposed Indians in the region to European diseases. In 1800 two-thirds of the Omaha Indian population was wiped out by smallpox. By 1804 three-fourths of the Ponca had died, too. The Oto lost so many people to disease that the group never recovered.

In the early 1800s, white people called the Great Plains the Great American Desert. The region wasn't actually a desert, but few trees grew on the prairie, and not much rain fell. In fact, most white Americans agreed that the land was too poor for themselves, so they reserved it for Indians. With a few exceptions, no white people were allowed to settle in the region. Instead this region was used only as a route to the West.

In 1812 Robert Stuart traveled eastward from the Pacific Coast of the Oregon Country to New York

City, 3,000 miles away. Stuart's party traveled along the Platte River and reached the Missouri River in the spring of 1813. For 50 years, pioneers going from the eastern part of the United States to Oregon followed Stuart's route—the Oregon Trail.

The Oregon Trail became like a highway in 1848, when gold was discovered in California. In 1850, 55,000 people crossed the Great Plains on their way to California, in hopes of striking it rich. The journey to the Pacific Coast took three months.

Chimney Rock was the Oregon Trail's most famous landmark. It could be seen for miles over the flat Nebraska plain.

By the 1850s, some people wanted to open the Great Plains to white settlement. To do this, the U.S. government would have to change the status of the region from Indian country to a U.S. territory. This happened in 1854, when the Kansas-Nebraska Act divided the Great Plains into the Kansas Territory to the south and the Nebraska Territory to the north.

By the time the territory was formed, most of the Indian tribes in eastern Nebraska had already given their lands to the U.S. government. Government officials escorted the Native Americans to **reservations,** areas of land set aside for Indian use.

But western Nebraska's Indians, such as the Sioux and Cheyenne, did not want to give up their lifestyles. Alarmed at the growing numbers of westbound pioneers, Indians attacked some travelers. In turn, U.S. soldiers attacked Indians. A period known as the Indian Wars continued from 1864 to 1879, when U.S. troops crushed the last Indian fighters. With their lives shattered, the remaining Indians were forced to live on reservations.

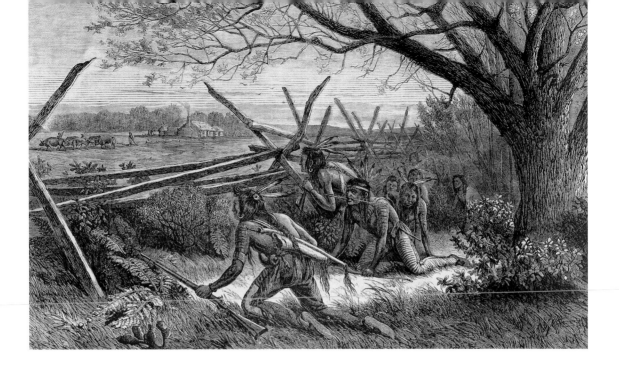

At this time, railroads were being built farther and farther west across North America. Both the Union Pacific and Burlington railroads tried to persuade Americans and even Europeans to come live in the Nebraska Territory. The railroads promised free land and successful farming in the territory. The more people there were in the region, the more shipping business the railroads were likely to get. The owners of the railroads would then be able to make more money.

Sioux Indians carried out several attacks on settlers. But eventually U.S. soldiers defeated the Sioux and forced them to live on reservations.

This advertisement from the Union Pacific Railroad *(right)* shows a map of the first cross-country track in the United States. For the first time, travelers could travel to the West along the Platte Valley *(below)*.

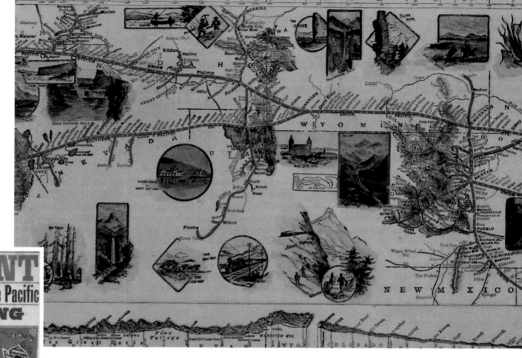

To persuade the railroads to lay tracks across the Great Plains, the U.S. government had given the companies huge chunks of land. By 1865 railroads owned more than one-seventh of Nebraska. The railroads made a fortune selling the land to settlers. U.S. citizens and European **immigrants** (newcomers) poured onto the prairie, and the railroads' owners got richer.

The Homestead Act of 1862 encouraged still more people to come to Nebraska. Settlers could claim 160 acres of government land for free. The new residents drew up a **constitution,** and on March 1, 1867, Nebraska became the 37th state to join the Union.

The immigrants had plenty of food on the prairie. They hunted prairie chickens, jackrabbits, antelope, ducks, and deer. Lamb's-quarter, wild lettuce, asparagus, currants, chokecherries, plums, and grapes were plentiful. Molasses, salt pork, and lard from the eastern United States added sugar, seasoning, and fat to the pioneers' diet.

Lumber was scarce on Nebraska's prairie, so early settlers built houses made of sod. Pioneers called these blocks of earth "Nebraska marble." Worms, bugs, and snakes often fell through the ceiling and into the house.

Prairie Fire!

In late summer, fire is a common threat on Nebraska's prairies—especially during dry years. Lightning, a spark from a campfire, or even sparks or heat from train wheels can easily light the dry grass, setting the plains ablaze.

The Indians taught Nebraska's settlers the only means of protection from prairie fires—a piece of ground without grass. The flames stop at these sections of land because there is nothing to catch fire. By digging a hole in the bare ground, people could also escape the intense heat. If they had time, farmers would rush to plow a strip of land around their homes to avoid losing all their possessions.

One tragedy occurred in 1873, when a fire swept toward a schoolhouse. The teacher cautioned everyone to stay with her on a piece of bare ground, but one mother insisted on taking some of the children home. The mother and 10 children died in the flames. Those who had stayed with the teacher survived the fire.

Grasshoppers can destroy an entire crop, leaving farmers with no means of food or income.

For pioneers in Nebraska, water was harder to find than food. The land close to rivers was the first to be claimed. Some farmers who lived far from rivers hired dowsers—people who used a special stick to find water underground. There was plenty of **groundwater** beneath Nebraska's surface.

In 1873 barbed wire was invented, and farmers had a cheap way to keep animals out of their fields. Fences don't stop insects, though. From 1874 to 1877, huge clouds of grasshoppers swarmed across the state, severely damaging Nebraska's crops—even the turnips and carrots growing underground. Hard times struck again in 1886 and 1887, when harsh winters killed most of the cattle in the state.

The weather could make pioneer life difficult in the summer, too. In July 1890, the temperature rose above 100 °F for 20 days. In 1894 three scorching days wiped out almost all of Nebraska's corn and wheat—the state's main crops.

To avoid losing everything during the next dry heat wave, Nebraskans began to **irrigate,** channeling water from the Platte River through ditches to their fields. Some farmers tried dryland farming. This method involved carefully preparing the soil. It was covered to seal in moisture and nutrients, and different crops were grown each year. Irrigation and dryland farming have saved thousands of crops since the drought of the 1890s.

In the early 1900s, farmers began to grow sugar beets, alfalfa, and potatoes. Crop prices tripled between 1910 and 1918, which meant good profits for farmers. In an effort to grow more and make more money, farmers borrowed money to buy more land. They spent the 1920s paying off the money they owed.

When drought returned to the Great Plains in the

1930s, Nebraska again looked like the Great American Desert. At night, the temperature sometimes actually rose! Huge clouds of dust darkened the sky as they swept across the plains, giving the region the nickname the Dust Bowl. Hundreds of farmers abandoned their land.

In the 1930s, some Great Plains dust storms were so severe they blocked out the sun. The dust storms carried away rich topsoil and left a coat of grime on everything.

At the end of the 1930s, the rains came back to the plains. But Nebraskans had learned from the years of hardship. They sought ways to increase the size of their harvests.

For example, farmers dug more irrigation ditches to carry water to their crops. And they started using chemical fertilizers to replace nutrients that wind and irrigation water carried from the fields. Farmers also began to plant stronger kinds of corn. They relied more and more on farm machinery to make their jobs easier and get higher crop yields.

In the 1930s and 1940s, Nebraska farmers began using new methods, including tractors and chemical fertilizers.

World War II (1939–1945) created a high demand for farm and manufactured products, boosting Nebraska's economy. In addition, more than 120,000 Nebraskans served in the military. Fort Robinson State Park became a prison for German soldiers captured during the war.

During World War II, many women in Nebraska worked in factories while the men went overseas to fight.

In 1963 the Nebraska legislature passed the Nebraska Educational Television Act, making the state one of the first in the country to broadcast educational programming to the entire state.

In 1974 Gerald R. Ford became the first Nebraska-born president of the United States. He served until

Gerald Ford on the campaign trail

1977. Nebraska's 1986 race for governor made U.S. history. It was the first election in which both major party candidates for the office of governor were women. Kay Orr, the Republican candidate, won the election.

The year 2000 was a difficult one for Nebraska's farmers. A severe drought destroyed crops, causing over one billion dollars in damage. Meanwhile, wildfires ravaged parts of the state, destroying over 200,000 acres of land. These setbacks bring to mind other tough times in Nebraska's history. But Nebraska's proud, hardworking citizens take pride in their ability to survive tough times, and they stand ready to conquer any challenge.

With about 400,000 people, Omaha is Nebraska's largest city.

PEOPLE & ECONOMY

Cornhuskers at Work and Play

Nebraska's 1.7 million people have close ties to their state and their fellow residents. Their ancestors came from different places, but Nebraskans have a common history of sharing Nebraska's land. And whether they work on farms, at stores, or in factories, Nebraskans still depend on the success of agriculture. A good year for farmers means a good year for the state.

Eastern Nebraska was the first part of the state to be plowed by early settlers, and that's where most Nebraskans still live. The main work then was farming. Now only 7 percent of Nebraskans work on a farms. And 78 percent of Nebraskans live in towns and cities, including Omaha, Lincoln (the state's capital), and Bellevue—the largest cities.

A pump pulls oil from a well. Oil was discovered in Nebraska in 1939.

But city dwellers in Nebraska still pay close attention to how well the state's farmers are doing. This is because many urban residents work in jobs that provide services for farmers.

For example, nearly one-fourth of the state's workers sell things, including grain and cattle from Nebraska's farms. Other people transport farm products by truck, train, or river barge to markets around the country. Many farm products from Nebraska are sold throughout the world.

About 11 percent of Nebraskans work in factories. Most handle agricultural products. Some workers process and package the state's crops. Millworkers in Omaha, Lincoln, and Fremont grind wheat and other

Modern farm equipment, like this combine, allows farmers to grow and harvest more crops than ever before.

Nebraska is America's second largest producer of cattle.

grains into flour for bread and pastries. In these three cities and in Schuyler, meat processors butcher hogs and cattle. Workers in Omaha and Lincoln make ice cream, butter, and other products from milk. The food companies that were the first in the country to turn out frozen dinners are located in Omaha.

Farmers who irrigate their land or who live in the eastern part of the state can grow corn, sorghum, and soybeans, which need a lot of water. Nebraska's corn harvest is the third largest in the United States. Corn is planted in more than 8 million acres of Nebraska's land each year. Much of this corn is used to feed farm animals.

Many farm animals eat sorghum, which is grown in the Platte River Valley.

Wheat, another major crop, is grown in the dry, western part of the state. This area is also where ranchers raise most of the state's beef cattle, which bring in more money than any other product in Nebraska.

Most of the Nebraskans who provide services to people or businesses work in or near Omaha or Lincoln. For example, Mutual of Omaha is one of the largest private health insurance companies in the world. A health insurance company promises, in exchange for regular payments, to pay for people's medical bills if they get hurt or sick.

About 14 percent of Nebraskans work for the government. Some government workers in Omaha report to Offutt Air Force Base.

Most of the state's small income from mining comes from oil wells in western and south central Nebraska. People who work in mines along the Platte and Republican Rivers dig and sell gravel and sand for making roads and buildings.

At Offutt Air Force Base, pilots prepare for a flight.

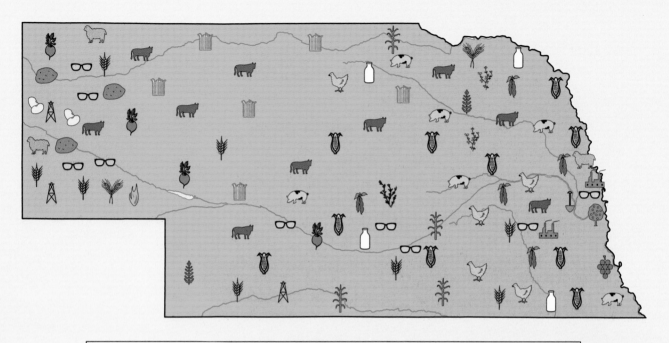

NEBRASKA
Economic Map

The symbols on this map show where different economic activities take place in Nebraska. The legend below explains what each symbol stands for.

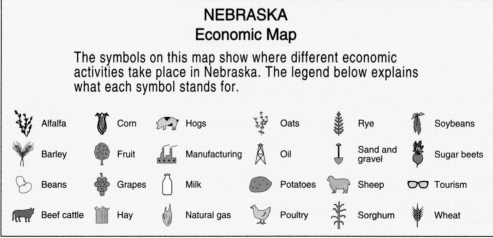

Alfalfa	Corn	Hogs	Oats	Rye	Soybeans
Barley	Fruit	Manufacturing	Oil	Sand and gravel	Sugar beets
Beans	Grapes	Milk	Potatoes	Sheep	Tourism
Beef cattle	Hay	Natural gas	Poultry	Sorghum	Wheat

These children are celebrating their heritage by dressing in the traditional costumes of their Czech ancestors.

Nebraskans represent a variety of ethnic backgrounds. But the majority—87 percent—have European ancestors. In the 1800s, railroad agents persuaded many Germans to come to Nebraska, and many people of German descent still live in the state. Other Nebraskans have ancestors who came from Sweden, Ireland, the Czech Republic, or Slovakia.

African Americans have lived in the state, mostly in cities and towns, since the early 1800s. They now make up about 4 percent of Nebraska's population. About 6 percent of Nebraskans are Latinos. The state also has a small number of Asian Americans.

Some Native American Nebraskans earn a living as farmers.

Only a small number of Native Americans still live in Nebraska. In 2000 fewer than 15,000 Indians lived in the state.

The lives and cultures of Indians, as well as pioneers, are celebrated in some of the artworks at the Joslyn Art Museum in Omaha. And Omaha's Great Plains Black History Museum details the lives of early African American cowboys, civic leaders, and other historical figures.

Omaha also features some museums devoted to children. At the Girls and Boys Town Hall of

History, visitors can learn about difficulties faced by some children and the social programs designed to help them. And the Children's Museum allows young people to try equipment for various professions, hobbies, and other activities. For dinosaur buffs, the State Museum at the University of Nebraska in Lincoln has a fine collection of fossils and woolly mammoth skeletons.

The Girls and Boys Town Hall of History tells the story of this well-known children's home.

Carhenge *(above)*, a replica of Stonehenge made out of old cars, is a favorite attraction for natives and tourists alike. It stands in a wheatfield north of Alliance, Nebraska.

The Nebraska Cornhuskers football team draws droves of fans to every game *(below)*.

The University of Nebraska also draws sports enthusiasts. When the school's football team has a Saturday game, a stadium packed with 76,000 cheering Cornhusker fans becomes the state's third largest city. Nebraskans are famous for their loyalty to this winning college team, which has won several national championships.

Nebraskans like to have fun outdoors. Several state parks offer trails for bicycling and horseback riding. And fishers, boaters, and swimmers enjoy the state's rivers and lakes.

In 1882 Buffalo Bill Cody started a Nebraskan tradition when he staged the "granddaddy of all American rodeos" in North Platte, Nebraska. A rodeo is still a favorite part of the town's yearly Nebraskaland Days, a week of fun every June. Modern-day cowboys can also participate in numerous other rodeos held throughout the state in the summertime.

Buffalo Bill Cody was one of Nebraska's most famous and colorful residents.

Rivers such as the Niobrara provide water for plants and people.

Saving Water Resources

I n a state that depends as heavily on farming as Nebraska does, water is an especially important resource. The first white pioneers settled along rivers. Once that land was taken up, newcomers discovered that if they dug deep enough, they would eventually reach an underground water supply. In fact, Nebraska lies over one of the largest underground water supplies in the nation. This source of water is named the Ogallala Aquifer.

Because Nebraska does not get much rain, people pump water out of the aquifer faster than rainwater seeps back into it. Almost all of the water used in Nebraska's homes and businesses comes from the ground. Farmers pump huge quantities to irrigate their fields.

Windmills pump water up from underground sources.

Rotating sprinklers, called irrigators, spray water over crops. The water is drawn from wells, most of which tap the Ogallala Aquifer, a natural underground storage space filled with water. This huge water supply provides water to eight states and stretches from Nebraska south across Kansas, Oklahoma, and Texas. Despite the aquifer's size, huge demand is draining the water faster than it is being replaced.

Residents have also drawn from surface water supplies, channeling water from the Platte and other rivers to farms and communities. As Nebraskans use up more and more of the state's water supplies, animals and plants that depend on this resource become threatened.

For example, the Platte River and the Rainwater Basin—a group of wetlands that stretch across 13 Nebraska counties—are part of the Central Flyway. This route is used by millions of migratory birds each spring and fall. These birds, which include ducks, geese, and sandhill cranes, have a much smaller area in which to rest and feed than they once did.

Pipes gush out water, flooding a field. This method of irrigation wastes water, and fewer farmers are using it.

Huge flocks of migrating birds visit the Rainwater Basin each year.

In the past, worms, snakes, frogs, and snails—food for the cranes—lived on vast plains that stretched along the Platte. Farmers plow, weed, and fertilize fields that line the Platte's banks, and cranes have difficulty getting enough food for the rest of their migration.

Dams in neighboring states cut down the flow of the Platte River by two-thirds before it even reaches Nebraska. So the Platte isn't nearly as wide as it used to be. Sandhill cranes can find only a few resting places that are safe from predators such as dogs, coyotes, and foxes.

Other places in Nebraska also suffer from a decreased water supply. The Rainwater Basin in south central Nebraska is drying up. For millions of years, rainwater and floodwaters from the Platte River have formed marshes in the basin, where many animals live.

The coyote preys on the birds of the Rainwater Basin, including sandhill cranes.

In the 1900s, however, farmers drained over four-fifths of the Rainwater Basin's original area for irrigation of crops. With less water in the Basin, birds and other marsh animals must crowd together. The added stress on ducks and geese causes thousands of birds to die each year of a disease called fowl cholera.

Various organizations in Nebraska are working to preserve the state's water supplies. Farmers have learned how to grow crops with less water. But some farmers resist efforts to save wetlands for wildlife. They say that wetlands are more valuable once they have been drained for farming because of the money that crops can earn.

Other Nebraskans, however, point out that by preserving wetlands, the state can earn money from visitors who come to view wildlife. And preserving water supplies is important for humans in the state, too. Nebraskans need water for everyday uses such as drinking water and plumbing. If Nebraskans continue to use water faster than nature can restock it, then one day none will be left.

With less water available, sandhill cranes must crowd closer and closer together.

Water is necessary for brushing teeth. By turning off the water while brushing, Nebraskans can help conserve water.

   All Nebraskans can help to conserve water. For example, people can take shorter showers, sprinkle the lawn for less time, and turn off the faucet while brushing their teeth. By doing these things, Nebraskans can help not only wildlife but also future generations of citizens.

In the year 2000, water and wildlife preservation received a big boost when they were included among the top four priorities of the Nebraska Environmental Trust. The trust, which receives money from state lottery income, chooses programs and projects that are geared toward preserving the state's natural resources. These include programs to protect Nebraska's surface and groundwater, and to restore habitat for the state's wilderness, including restoring wetlands. Nebraskans take pride in the beauty of their state's natural wonders and are working hard to preserve them for generations to come.

ALL ABOUT NEBRASKA

Fun Facts

Kool-Aid was developed in Hastings, Nebraska, in 1927. It is the state's official soft drink.

Nebraska is the only state in the nation with a unicameral (one house) legislature. All other states have two-house legislatures, with a senate and a house of representatives. Nebraska's system was adopted in 1937.

Lincoln, Nebraska, is home to the world's only museum of roller skating. The National Museum of Roller Skating features the world's largest collection of historical roller skates, dating from 1819.

The National Museum of Roller Skating honors Fred Murree, a professional skater and Pawnee Indian from Nebraska. Murree performed on skates until he was 82 years old!

The 911 emergency communication system was developed and first introduced in Lincoln, Nebraska.

The largest planted forest in the United States is in Nebraska. Covering about 22,000 acres, the trees are part of the Nebraska National Forest.

Before it was the Cornhusker State, Nebraska was called the Bug-Eating State because of its many nighthawks, which are birds that eat lots of insects.

The world's first rodeo was held at North Platte, Nebraska, in July 1882 and starred its founder, William Frederick "Buffalo Bill" Cody.

The world's largest fossil of a woolly mammoth was found in Nebraska. It is 13 feet, 4 inches high.

STATE SONG

Nebraska's state song was written in 1960 by Jim Fras. An immigrant from Russia, Fras was inspired to write the song while lying in a pasture. The song was officially adopted in 1967.

BEAUTIFUL NEBRASKA

Words by Jim Fras and Guy G. Miller; music by Jim Fras

Beau-ti-ful Ne-bra-ska, peace-ful prai-rie land. Laced with ma-ny ri-vers and the hills of sand; Dark green val-leys

cra-dled in the earth, Rain and sun-shine bring a-bun-dant birth. Beau-ti-ful Ne-bra-ska, as you look a-round,

You will find a rain-bow rea-ching to the ground; All these won-ders by the Mas-ter's hand; Beau-ti-ful Ne-bra-ska

land. We are so proud of this state where we live, There is no

place that has so much to give. Beau-ti-ful Ne-bra-ska, as you look a-round, you will find a rain-bow

rea-ching to the ground; All these won-ders by the Mas-ter's hand. Beau-ti-ful Ne-bra-ska land.

You can hear "Nebraska" by visiting this website:
<http://www.50states.com/songs/nebraska.htm>

A NEBRASKA RECIPE

Corn is Nebraska's most important crop.
And there's no more delicious way to enjoy
this grain than by making it into a moist and
sweet bread. This simple recipe for corn bread
muffins makes a tasty addition to any breakfast, lunch,
or dinner. And muffins go great with another major Nebraska
crop—honey! Ask an adult to help with all steps involving an oven.

CORN BREAD MUFFINS

½ cup butter, softened

⅔ cup sugar

¼ cup honey

2 eggs

½ teaspoon salt

1½ cups flour

¾ cup corn meal

½ teaspoon baking powder

½ cup milk

8 oz. frozen corn kernels, thawed

1. Ask an adult to preheat oven to 400 °F. Grease 12-cup muffin pan.
2. In large bowl, cream together butter, sugar, honey, eggs, and salt. Mix in flour, corn meal, and baking powder. Blend thoroughly. Stir in milk and corn.
3. Pour batter into muffin cups.
4. Bake in preheated oven for 20 to 25 minutes, or until toothpick inserted in center of muffin comes out clean.

Makes 12 muffins.

HISTORICAL TIMELINE

8000 B.C.   The first humans enter the area that would later become Nebraska.

A.D. 1400   Dust storms sweep across the Great Plains.

1600   Plains Indians begin using horses to hunt bison.

1739   Paul and Pierre Mallet travel along the Platte River in the area that became Nebraska.

1803   France sells the territory that includes the area that later became Nebraska to the United States in a deal called the Louisiana Purchase.

1804   Lewis and Clark pass through the Nebraska area on their historic journey through western North America.

1807   Manuel Lisa builds the first fur-trading post in the Nebraska area.

1854   The Kansas-Nebraska Act divides the Great Plains into two territories.

1864   The Indian Wars begin and continue until 1879.

1867   Nebraska enters the Union as the 37th state.

1874 The first of several grasshopper swarms severely damages Nebraska's crops.

1917 The United States enters World War I (1914–1918). Almost 50,000 Nebraskan men serve in the U.S. armed forces.

1930 A decade of drought and severe dust storms begins to ravage Nebraska.

1937 Nebraska becomes the first U.S. state with a unicameral (one-house) legislature.

1941 The United States enters World War II (1939–1945). Nebraska manufacturing plants produce more than $1.2 billion worth of war supplies.

1948 The Strategic Air Command establishes its base for the defense of North America at Offutt Air Force Base near Omaha.

1949 Oil fields are discovered in western Nebraska.

1963 The Educational Television Act is passed, making Nebraska one of the first states to broadcast educational programming to the entire state.

1970 More than 60 percent of Nebraskans live in cities.

1986 Kay Orr becomes the first woman Republican governor in U.S. history.

2000 Severe droughts cause an estimated $1 billion in damages.

OUTSTANDING NEBRASKANS

Clarence William (C.W.) Anderson

Clarence William (C.W.) Anderson (1891–1971) was an author who also illustrated books about horses. Born in Wahoo, Nebraska, he became famous for his *Billy and Blaze* series. Anderson's own first horse, Bobcat, was a model for some of the horses in the books.

Fred Astaire

Fred Astaire (1899–1987) danced and acted with a style that made him a star all over the world. Astaire was born in Omaha and began his career dancing with his sister Adele. He appeared in more than 30 film musicals, including 10 with his famous dance partner, Ginger Rogers.

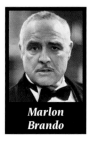

Marlon Brando

Marlon Brando (born 1924), a native of Omaha, is a world-famous actor. Known for his good looks and rough, slurred speech, Brando won Academy Awards for his roles in the films *On the Waterfront* and *The Godfather.*

William Jennings Bryan (1860–1925) moved to Lincoln in 1887 and served as a representative from Nebraska in the U.S. Congress. He ran for president three times but never won. Known as one of the greatest speakers of his time, Bryan worked to improve the lives of farmers and influenced people all over the nation.

William Jennings Bryan

Johnny Carson (born 1925) is one of America's best-loved television personalities. He began performing at a young age, putting on magic shows and acting in plays. Born in Iowa, Carson grew up in Norfolk, Nebraska. He got his first broadcasting job in Lincoln. He hosted *The Tonight Show* on television from 1962 to 1992.

Willa Sibert Cather (1873–1947), an author, moved from Virginia to Nebraska at the age of 10. Several of her novels tell of the pioneer Midwest, including *O Pioneers!* and *My Ántonia*. The novel *One of Ours* won Cather a Pulitzer Prize in 1923.

Willa Sibert Cather

William Frederick ("Buffalo Bill") Cody (1846–1917), a legend of the "wild west," started his career as a field hand when he was nine. He went on to become a scout, buffalo hunter, showman, Pony Express rider, and actor. A native of Iowa, Buffalo Bill staged the first American rodeo in North Platte, Nebraska.

Buffalo Bill Cody

Crazy Horse (Tashunca-Uitco) (1844?–1877), an Oglala Sioux chief, tried to recapture Indian lands from the United States. He led his people in raids on white settlements and warred against U.S. Army troops. Crazy Horse was killed while being forced into a jail cell in Camp Robinson, Nebraska.

Edward Joseph Flanagan (1886–1948), a Roman Catholic priest, was born in Ireland. He founded Father Flanagan's Home for Boys in Omaha. The home became Boys Town in 1922. More than 8,500 mistreated and disabled boys and girls are helped every year by the organization, which later became Girls and Boys Town.

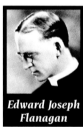

Edward Joseph Flanagan

Henry Fonda (1905–1982) was an actor born in Grand Island, Nebraska. Fonda's film career spanned six decades—from the 1930s to the 1980s. He appeared in more than 80 films, including *The Grapes of Wrath*, *Mister Roberts*, and *On Golden Pond*, for which he won an Academy Award in 1981. He is the father of actors Jane and Peter Fonda, and the grandfather of actor Bridget Fonda.

Henry Fonda

Gerald R. Ford

Gerald R. Ford (born 1913) was the only Nebraska-born president of the United States. Appointed vice president under President Richard Nixon in December 1973, he took office upon Nixon's resignation in August 1974. A Republican, Ford served as president until 1977, losing the 1976 election to Jimmy Carter.

Bob Gibson

Bob Gibson (born 1935) was a pitcher for the Saint Louis Cardinals from 1959 to 1975. Born in Omaha, Gibson was known for his blazing fastball and intimidating style of pitching. He won the National League Cy Young Award for best pitcher in 1968 and 1970. He was inducted into the Baseball Hall of Fame in 1981.

Malcolm X

Malcolm X (Malcolm Little) (1925–1965), a religious and civil rights leader, was born in Omaha. He joined the Black Muslim organization and encouraged African Americans to take pride in their race and their achievements. A powerful and inspiring speaker, he led a movement to unite black people all over the world. He believed that blacks should have a separate American nation. Malcolm X was assassinated in New York City on February 21, 1965.

Julius Sterling Morton (1832–1902) was a newspaper editor who started a special day for planting trees, Arbor Day, which has become a national holiday. Morton moved to Nebraska when he was 22 years old. A lover of trees and agriculture, he began planting trees around his treeless yard and town.

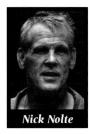

Nick Nolte

Nick Nolte (born 1941) is an actor who has starred in many popular films, including *48 Hrs., Down and Out in Beverly Hills,* and *The Prince of Tides*—for which he received an Academy Award nomination. He was born in Omaha.

George Norris (1861–1944), a native of Ohio, represented Nebraska in the U.S. Congress for 40 years. He convinced the government to provide electricity to rural areas. He also gave money to Nebraska's farmers in times of drought.

George Norris

Tom Osborne (born 1937) was coach of the University of Nebraska Cornhuskers football team from 1973 to 1998, winning 13 conference titles and three national championships. A teacher with degrees in educational psychology, Osborne was elected to the U.S. House of Representatives in 2000.

Susan LaFlesche Picotte (1865–1915) was the first Native American woman to earn a medical degree. She devoted her life to improving Indian health care on the Omaha Reservation in northeastern Nebraska, where she grew up.

Red Cloud

Red Cloud (Mahpiua Luta) (1822–1909) was a war leader for the Oglala Sioux. Born in Nebraska, Red Cloud tried to stop the opening of the Bozeman Trail, which ran through Indian hunting grounds in Wyoming and Montana. He eventually signed a peace treaty and lived on a reservation named for him.

Mari Sandoz

Mari Sandoz (1900–1966), an author, was born in Sheridan County, Nebraska. She wrote about the lives of Indians, ranchers, and homesteaders in *Love Song to the Plains*, a history of Nebraska. She also wrote two children's books about Sioux life.

Robert Taylor (1911–1969) a Hollywood film star, was named Arlington Spangler Brugh when he was born in Filley, Nebraska. Taylor's good looks and charm attracted crowds to his films from the 1930s through the 1950s. His films include *Knights of the Round Table*, *Bataan*, and *Magnificent Obsession*.

Robert Taylor

FACTS-AT-A-GLANCE

Nickname: Cornhusker State

Song: "Beautiful Nebraska"

Motto: Equality Before the Law

Flower: goldenrod

Tree: cottonwood

Bird: western meadowlark

Fossil: mammoth

Gem: blue agate

Insect: honeybee

Date and ranking of statehood:
    March 1, 1867, the 37th state

Capital: Lincoln

Area: 76,878 square miles

Rank in area, nationwide: 15th

Average January temperature: 23° F

Average July temperature: 76° F

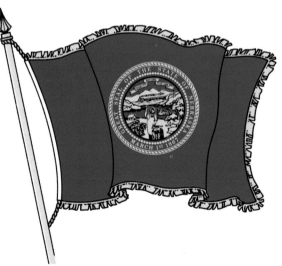

The Nebraska flag shows the Nebraska state seal on a field of blue. The flag has been in use since 1925.

POPULATION GROWTH

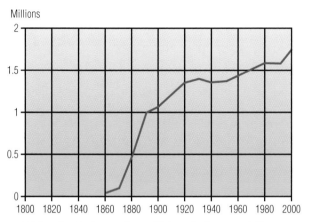

Millions

This chart shows how Nebraska's population has grown from 1860 to 2000.

Nebraska's state seal features a smith with hammer and anvil, symbolizing Nebraska's industry. The settler's cabin and bales of wheat represent Nebraska's commitment to agriculture. Nebraska's motto is at the top of the seal.

Population: 1,711,263 (2000 census)

Rank in population, nationwide: 38th

Major cities and populations: (2000 census) Omaha (390,007), Lincoln (225,581), Bellevue (44,382), Grand Island (42,940), Kearney (27,431)

U.S. senators: 2

U.S. representatives: 3

Electoral votes: 5

Natural resources: clay, gravel, limestone, natural gas, petroleum, sand, soil

Agricultural products: alfalfa, beans, beef cattle, corn, hay, hogs, honey, milk, potatoes, sorghum, soybeans, sugar beets, wheat

Manufactured goods: chemicals, electronic equipment, farm equipment, food products, machinery, metal products

WHERE NEBRASKANS WORK

Services—63 percent (services includes jobs in trade; community, social, and personal services; finance, insurance and real estate; transportation, communication, and utilities)

Government—14 percent

Manufacturing—11 percent

Agriculture—7 percent

Construction—5 percent

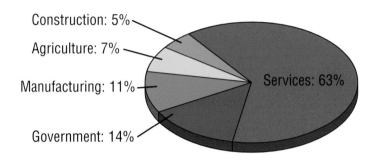

Construction: 5%
Agriculture: 7%
Manufacturing: 11%
Government: 14%
Services: 63%

GROSS STATE PRODUCT

Services—57 percent

Manufacturing—14 percent

Government—13 percent

Agriculture—12 percent

Construction—4 percent

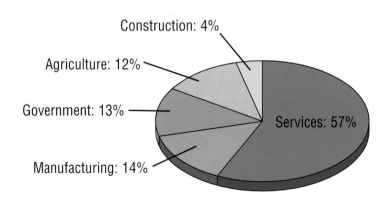

Construction: 4%
Agriculture: 12%
Government: 13%
Services: 57%
Manufacturing: 14%

NEBRASKA WILDLIFE

Mammals: antelope, badger, beaver, bighorn sheep, bison, bobcat, coyote, elk, fox, mule deer, muskrat, prairie dog, raccoon, skunk, squirrel, white-tailed deer

Birds: ducks, geese, grouse, pheasants, quail, sandhill cranes

Amphibians and reptiles: frogs, lizards, salamanders, snakes, toads, turtles

Fish: bass, carp, catfish, crappie, perch, pike, trout, walleye

Trees: ash, box elder, cedar, cottonwood, elm, linden, locust, oak, pine, walnut, willow

Wild plants: blueflag, bluestem, buffalo grass, chokecherry, columbine, goldenrod, grama, larkspur, phlox, poppy, primrose, spiderwort, sunflower, violets, wild plum, wild rose

Elk

PLACES TO VISIT

Agate Fossil Beds National Monument, near Harrison
This site brings the visitor a long way back in time—19 million years! That's the age of some of the fossils in this historic spot. Other exhibits feature more recent plants and animals of the region, and a large collection of Native American artifacts.

Chimney Rock National Historic Site, near Bayard
This 500-foot-high chimney-shaped rock formation has been an important landmark for travelers since the days of the Oregon Trail. The site's visitor center features displays on how the rock was formed and an interactive exhibit that gives kids a chance to step into the shoes of Oregon Trail travelers.

Girls and Boys Town, near Omaha
Visit the place where thousands of young boys and girls have been given a second chance in life. Founded in 1917 by Father Edward J. Flanagan, Girls and Boys Town offers food, clothing, shelter, education, spiritual guidance, and medical care to homeless, neglected, and abused children. Stop at the Hall of History to learn about the organization's rich history.

Great Platte River Road Archway Monument, Kearney
This attraction, opened in 2000, is home to an exciting interactive exhibit that follows the history of the Platte River as a cross-country travel route. It includes realistic displays of the Oregon Trail, Pony Express, transcontinental railroad and the modern Eisenhower Interstate Highway System.

Henry Doorly Zoo, Omaha

Each year over a million people visit this zoo. Covering over 104 acres, the zoo features the world's largest enclosed rainforest, an aviary where exotic birds fly free, an aquarium, an IMAX theater, and North America's largest wildcat exhibit.

Joslyn Art Museum, Omaha

One of Omaha's finest attractions, this museum houses one of the world's most impressive collections of Western American art. The pink marble structure is itself a work of art and one of the most recognizable buildings in the state.

Lake McConaughy and Lake Ogallala, north of Ogallala

Enjoy sailing, jetskiing, scuba diving, camping, sailboarding, and fishing in gigantic, 22-mile-long Lake McConaughy. Lake Ogallala is smaller, but it features Kingsley Dam, the second largest hydraulic-filled dam in the world.

Scotts Bluff National Monument, near Gering

This famous Oregon Trail landmark was named after a fur trader who died there. The monument's visitor center features exhibits about the trail, early fur traders, and the Pony Express. Ruts from Oregon Trail wagons are still visible in the area.

Strategic Air and Space Museum, near Ashland

This museum is dedicated to preserving the history of the Strategic Air Command (SAC), the organization of the U.S. Air Force dedicated to fighting nuclear war. The museum features aircraft, missiles, and other equipment used in defense of the nation, as well as educational programs focused on aviation and aerospace topics.

ANNUAL EVENTS

Children's Groundwater Festival, Grand Island—*March*

Annual Migration, Hastings—*April*

Arbor Day, Nebraska City—*April*

Armed Forces Day, Ashland—*May*

Mother's Day Tea, Ainsworth—*May*

Buffalo Bill Rodeo, North Platte—*June*

Czech Festival, Hastings—*June*

Nebraskaland Days, North Platte—*June*

Old Man River Days, Peru—*June*

Fur Trade Days, Chadron—*July*

Oregon Trail Days, Gering—*July*

Nebraska State Fair, Lincoln—*August–September*

Toucan Open, Lake McConaughy—*September*

Vocair Flying Club's Annual Fly-In Breakfast, Sidney—*October*

Star City Holiday Parade, Lincoln—*December*

LEARN MORE ABOUT NEBRASKA

BOOKS

General

Bjorklund, Ruth. *Nebraska.* New York: Benchmark Books, 2002. For older readers.

Fradin, Dennis Brindell. *Nebraska.* Chicago: Children's Press, 1995.

McNair, Sylvia. *Nebraska.* New York: Children's Press, 1999. For older readers.

Special Interest

Benson, Michael. *Malcolm X.* Minneapolis, MN: Lerner Publications Company, 2002. This biography follows the life of Malcolm X, the African American civil rights leader, who was born in Omaha. For older readers.

Bowen, Andy Russell. *The Back of Beyond: A Story about Lewis and Clark.* Minneapolis, MN: Carolrhoda Books, Inc., 1997. Follow the adventures of Lewis and Clark as they explore the wilderness of the western United States.

Streissguth, Tom. *Writer of the Plains: A Story about Willa Cather.* Minneapolis, MN: Carolrhoda Books, Inc., 1997. A biography of Willa Cather, the Nebraskan Pulitzer Prize-winning author.

Toht, David W. *Sodbuster.* Minneapolis, MN: Lerner Publications Company, 1996. Experience the challenging lives of the settlers of the open plains in the early 1800s.

Fiction

Bunting, Eve. *Dandelions.* San Diego, CA: Harcourt Brace & Company, 1995. Young Zoe and her family make a home for themselves in the wild Nebraska prairie.

Gray, Dianne E. *Holding Up the Earth.* New York: Houghton Mifflin Company, 2000. Fourteen-year-old Hope visits her new foster mother's Nebraska farm and gets a picture of the past through old letters, a diary, and stories of four girls who lived there years ago.

Murphy, Jim. *My Face to the Wind: The Diary of Sarah Jane Price, a Prairie Teacher.* New York: Scholastic, Inc., 2001. Teenager Sarah Jane records her experiences as a schoolteacher in the 1880s.

Ruckman, Ivy. *In Care of Cassie Tucker.* New York: Delacorte Press, 1998. Eleven-year-old Cassie has a lot to cope with when her teenage cousin comes to move in with her and her family on her Nebraska farm in 1899.

WEBSITES

Nebraska Online: The Official Website for the State of Nebraska
<http://www.state.ne.us>
Nebraska's official website provides information on the state's agricultural and natural resources, business, education, health and safety. It also offers facts about Nebraska and its history.

Nebraska Division of Travel and Tourism
<http://www.visitnebraska.org/>
The state's official tourism website has links to the sites of many of the state's most popular attractions, as well as lists of events, current Nebraska weather information, and facts about the state's history, people, culture, and natural resources.

Omaha World-Herald Online Edition
< http://www.omaha.com/>
Read Omaha's major daily newspaper on the Internet.

Huskers Online: The Official Site of Nebraska Athletics
<http://www.huskers.com/>
Get all the information you need about Nebraska Cornhuskers athletics, including current news on the school's powerhouse football team.

PRONUNCIATION GUIDE

Apache (uh-PACH-ee)

Cheyenne (shy-AN)

loess (LESS)

Loup (LOOP)

Mallet, Pierre (mah-LAY, pee-AIR)

McConaughy (muh-KAHN-uh-hay)

Niobrara (ny-uh-BRAHR-uh)

Ogallala Aquifer (oh-guh-LAHL-uh AK-weh-fur)

Oto (OH-doh)

Pawnee (paw-NEE)

Platte (PLAT)

Ponca (PAHNG-kuh)

Sioux (SOO)

For years, Nebraskan ranchers have upheld the curious tradition of placing their boots over fence posts.

GLOSSARY

constitution: the system of basic laws or rules of a government, society, or organization; the document in which these laws or rules are written

drought: a long period of extreme dryness due to lack of rain or snow

glacier: a large body of ice and snow that moves slowly over land

groundwater: water that lies beneath the earth's surface. The water comes from rain and snow that seep through soil into the cracks and other openings in rocks. Groundwater supplies wells and springs.

hydropower: the electricity produced by using waterpower; also called hydro-electric power

immigrant: a person who moves into a foreign country and settles there

irrigate: to water land by directing water through canals, ditches, pipes, or sprinklers

loess: fine-grained soil or dust that is carried by wind and deposited on the ground

marshland: a spongy wetland soaked with water for long periods of time. Marshland is usually treeless. Grasses are the main form of vegetation found in marshland.

prairie: a large area of level or gently rolling grassy land with few trees

reservation: public land set aside by the government to be used by Native Americans

till: a mixture of clay, sand, and gravel dragged along by a glacier and left behind when the ice melts

INDEX

PHOTO ACKNOWLEDGMENTS

COVER: © James L. Amos/CORBIS (left;) © Reuters NewMedia Inc./CORBIS (right); © Layne Kennedy/CORBIS pp. 2–3; © D. Robert & Lorri Franz/CORBIS, p. 3; © M. Angelo/CORBIS, pp. 4 (detail), 7 (detail), 16 (detail), 39 (detail), 51 (detail); U.S. Fish and Wildlife Service, pp. 6, 54; © James L. Amos/CORBIS, p. 10; © Philip Gould/CORBIS, p. 11; Kent & Donna Dannen, pp. 12, 15 (both), 52 (bottom), 80; Merrilee Thomas, p. 13; © Stan Strange / Root Resources, p. 14; Smithsonian Institution photo #80-1819, p. 17; Lincoln Convention and Visitors Bureau, p. 18; © John Cunningham/Visuals Unlimited, pp. 19, 23; Independent Picture Service, pp. 20, 36, 67 (top); © Lowell Georgia/Photo Researchers, Inc., p. 21; Nebraska Department of Economic Development, pp. 22, 49; Harper's Weekly, November 2, 1867, Oregon Historical Society, OrHi 23551 (tinted), p. 25; Library of Congress, pp. 27, 33, 66 (bottom); Nebraska State Historical Society, pp. 30, 67 (second from top), 69 (top, second from bottom); Union Pacific Museum Collection, p. 28 (both); Solomon P. Butcher Collection, Nebraska State Historical Society, p. 29; © R. Culentine / Visuals Unlimited, p. 31; © Gehl Company/CORBIS, p. 34; © CORBIS, pp. 35, 43; © Morton Beebe/CORBIS, p. 38; Steve Cathcart, Southwest Nebraska Convention and Visitors Bureau, p. 39; Doyen Salsig, pp. 40, 41, 42; Lambert Slepicka, p. 45; Jeff Greenberg, p. 46; Girls and Boys Town, pp. 47, 67 (second from bottom); © Tom Bean/CORBIS, p. 48 (left); University of Nebraska, Lincoln, p. 48 (right); © Jim Steinberg/Photo Researchers, Inc., p. 50; Nebraska Game and Parks, p. 51; Phyllis Cerny, p. 52 (top); Nebraska Natural Resources Commission, Terry L. Cartwright, photographer, p. 53; © Tom and Pat Leeson/Photo Researchers Inc., p. 55; © Arthur Morris/Visuals Unlimited, p. 57; © Jeff Greenberg/ Visuals Unlimited, p. 58; National Museum of Roller Skating, p. 60; Jack Lindstrom, p. 61; Macmillan Publishing Company, p. 66 (top); Hollywood Book & Poster, pp. 66 (second from top, second from bottom), 67 (bottom), 68 (bottom), 69 (bottom); The White House, p. 68 (top); © Bettmann/CORBIS, p.68 (second from top); AP/Wide World Photos, p. 68 (second from bottom); Smithsonian Institution National Anthropological Archives, Bureau of American Enthnology Collection, p. 69 (second from top, neg. #3237-A); Jean Matheny, p. 70 (top); © D. Dvorak Jr., p. 73.